C000146204

Maritime Terrorism in Southeast Asia: The Abu Sayyaf Threat

Rommel C. Banlaoi

The BiblioGov Project is an effort to expand awareness of the public documents and records of the U.S. Government via print publications. In broadening the public understanding of government and its work, an enlightened democracy can grow and prosper. Ranging from historic Congressional Bills to the most recent Budget of the United States Government, the BiblioGov Project spans a wealth of government information. These works are now made available through an environmentally friendly, print-on-demand basis, using only what is necessary to meet the required demands of an interested public. We invite you to learn of the records of the U.S. Government, heightening the knowledge and debate that can lead from such publications.

Included are the following Collections:

Budget of The United States Government
Presidential Documents
United States Code
Education Reports from ERIC
GAO Reports
History of Bills
House Rules and Manual
Public and Private Laws

Code of Federal Regulations
Congressional Documents
Economic Indicators
Federal Register
Government Manuals
House Journal
Privacy act Issuances
Statutes at Large

Rommel C. Banlaoi is professor of political science at the National Defense College of the Philippines (NDCP), where he served as Vice President for Administrative Affairs from 1998 to 2002. He is presently the course director of Political Dimension of National Security at NDCP. He provides consulting services to the Philippine Department of National Defense and the League of Municipalities of the Philippines, as well as acting as executive director of the Strategic and Integrative Studies Center, Inc.

He has served as a visiting scholar, research fellow, professor, lecturer, or instructor at the Centre of Asian Studies of the University of Hong Kong; the Institute for Asia Pacific Studies of the Chinese Academy of Social Sciences, Beijing; the Institute of Southeast Asian Studies of Zhongshan University, Guangzhou, China; the Asia Pacific Center for Security Studies, Honolulu; the Faculty of Law, Leiden University, the Netherlands; De La Salle University in Manila; University of the Philippines Center for Integrative and Development Studies; and the University of the Philippines in Los Banos. He has also lectured at the Joint Command and Staff College, Army Command and Staff College, Naval Command and Staff College, Air Command and Staff College, and Foreign Service Institute, all based in the Philippines.

Professor Banlaoi is editor, author, or coauthor of five books, two monographs, and numerous refereed articles and book chapters. His latest book is War on Terrorism in Southeast Asia *(October 2004), published by Rex Book Store International. He is presently finishing his PhD in political science at the University of the Philippines, where he obtained his BA and MA in political science.*

© 2005 by Rommel C. Banlaoi
Naval War College Review, Autumn 2005, Vol. 58, No. 4

MARITIME TERRORISM IN SOUTHEAST ASIA

The Abu Sayyaf Threat

Rommel C. Banlaoi

S outheast Asia is fast becoming the world's maritime terrorism hot spot, because of a very high incidence of piracy and a burgeoning threat of terrorism.
Southeast Asia is the region most prone to acts of piracy, accounting for around
50 percent of all attacks worldwide. This situation is aggravated by indigenous
terrorist groups with strong maritime traditions. The growing nexus between
piracy and terrorism makes maritime terrorism in Southeast Asia a regional security concern.

The Abu Sayyaf Group (ASG), the Gerakan Aceh Merdeka (GAM), and the
Jemaah Islamiyah (JI) are three terrorist groups in Southeast Asia with the in-
tention and proven capability to wage maritime terrorism. Of these groups, Abu
Sayyaf is the best known but least understood.[1]

This article addresses the threat of maritime terrorism in Southeast Asia, with
emphasis on the ASG—its organizational structure, membership, and strategy,
and its implications for maritime security in Southeast Asia.

THE NEXUS BETWEEN PIRACY AND TERRORISM

The International Maritime Bureau (IMB) reported in 2003 that out of 445 ac-
tual and attempted pirate attacks on merchant ships, 189 attacks occurred in
Southeast Asian waters, 121 of them in the Indonesian Archipelago and
thirty-five around Malaysia and Singapore, particularly in the congested Strait
of Malacca.[2] The 2003 figure represented an increase of thirty-three attacks in
the region over the preceding year. Pirate attacks in Southeast Asian waters were
much more frequent than in Africa or Latin America. In 2004, the IMB reported
that pirate attacks dropped to 325, but Southeast Asia continued to top the list.

Out of the total pirate attacks worldwide in 2004, the IMB recorded ninety-three in Indonesian waters alone. A worrisome IMB report states that pirates preying on shipping were more violent than ever in 2004, murdering a total of thirty crew members, compared with twenty-one in 2003.[3]

Because piracy is frequent in Southeast Asia, terrorists have found it an attractive cover for maritime terrorism. Though the motives of pirates and terrorists are different (the former pursues economic gains while the latter advances political objectives),[4] terrorists could adopt pirate tactics of stealing a ship, which they could then blow up or ram into another vessel or a port facility, to sow fear. Thus, security experts consider the line between piracy and terrorism to have blurred in Southeast Asia: "Not only do pirates terrorize ships' crews, but terror groups like al-Qaeda could also use pirates' methods either to attack ships, or to seize ships to use in terror attacks at megaports, much like the Sept. 11 hijackers used planes."[5] A more sinister scenario is that a small but lethal biological weapon could be smuggled into a harbor aboard ship and released.[6] Terrorist groups regard seaports and international cruise lines as attractive targets, because they lie in the intersection of terrorist intent, capability, and opportunity.[7]

The growth of commercial shipping in Southeast Asia makes the challenge of piracy and maritime terrorism in the region alarming. Since 1999 the U.S. Coast Guard Intelligence Coordinating Center has forecast that world commercial shipping will increase enormously by 2020 and that this will trigger the proliferation of transnational crime and terrorism at sea.[8] It has also forecast that growth in the cruise-line industry and the emergence of high-speed ferries will be key developments in the maritime passenger transport business through 2020.[9]

Shipping has long been the major form of transport connecting Southeast Asia to the rest of the world.[10] Four of the world's busiest shipping routes are in Southeast Asia: the Malacca, Sunda, Lombok, and Makassar straits.[11] Every year more than 50 percent of the world's annual merchant fleet tonnage transits these straits, and more than 15 percent of the value of world trade passes through Southeast Asia.[12] These figures are projected to grow unless major disasters occur in the region.

The Malacca Strait alone carries more than a quarter of the world's maritime trade each year—more than fifty thousand large ships pass, including forty to fifty tankers.[13] Because the strait is the maritime gateway between the Indian Ocean and the Pacific Ocean, it will remain a world center of maritime activity. It has been argued that it would be difficult for terrorists to disrupt shipping in the strait by sinking a ship in a precise spot.[14] However, were terrorists to hijack one and turn it to a floating bomb to destroy ports or oil refineries, the effect would be catastrophic. Such an attack incident would not only cripple world trade and slow down international shipping but spread fear—more broadly than on 9/11. The prospect of such a maritime incident is not remote. Container shipping is highly vulnerable, and the possibility of its use as a weapon of mass destruction has been documented.[15] Thus, maritime terrorism in Southeast Asia must prudently be considered no longer a question of if, but rather of when and where.[16] One maritime security analyst goes farther—that maritime terrorism in Southeast Asia is not even a question of when but of how often and what we are going to do about it.[17]

Maritime terrorism in Southeast Asia is all the more serious a regional security concern because al-Qa'ida and its operatives have a keen awareness of maritime trade and understand its significance to the global economy.[18] Al-Qa'ida knows the impact of maritime terrorist attacks on shipping and has therefore planned to carry out acts of maritime terrorism.[19]

Al-Qa'ida's capability to do so has already been demonstrated by suicide attacks on the destroyer USS *Cole* (DDG 67) in 2000 and the French tanker *Limburg* in 2002. Fifteen cargo ships are believed to be owned by al-Qa'ida, which could use them for terrorist attacks.[20] Al-Qa'ida operatives are also being trained in diving, with a view to attacking ships from below.[21]

Southeast Asia has already experienced maritime terrorism. In the Strait of Malacca, for example, Aegis Defense Services, a London-based security organization, has reported that the robbery of a chemical tanker, the *Dewi Madrim*, appeared to be the work of terrorists "who were learning how to steer a ship, in preparation for a future attack at sea."[22] In Singapore, intelligence and law enforcement forces have uncovered a Jemaah Islamiyah plot to bomb the U.S. naval facility there. The sinister linking of terrorists and pirates has made Southeast Asia a focal point of maritime fear.[23] It is for this reason that the Singapore home affairs minister, Wong Kan Seng, declared in 2003 that pirates roaming the waters of Southeast Asia should be regarded as outright terrorists.[24] In an interview, the minister argued, "Although we talk about piracy or anti-piracy, if there's a crime conducted at sea sometimes we do not know whether it's pirates or terrorists who occupy the ship so we have to treat them all alike."[25]

ABU SAYYAF AND MARITIME TERRORISM

One terrorist group that has developed a capability to wage maritime terrorism in Southeast Asia is the Abu Sayyaf Group. Various analysts have already discussed its historical and financial ties with al-Qa'ida.[26] Yet little is known about its organizational structure, strategy, tactics, or maritime terrorist capabilities.

The Early Years and Historical Roots

Originally called Mujahideen Commando Freedom Fighters (MCFF), Abu Sayyaf was organized in the Philippines as an underground militant Muslim group in the early 1990s by the late Ustadz Abdurajak Janjalani, who was recognized as its overall "amir."[27] Janjalani founded the ASG in the context of a global and regional Islamic resurgence.[28] A veteran of the Afghan-Soviet war, Janjalani had developed a close friendship with Osama Bin Laden and Ramzi Yousef in the early 1980s while in Peshawar, Pakistan. Yousef was the mastermind of the "Bojinka plot" to bomb eleven American jetliners and to assassinate Pope John Paul II during a visit to Manila in 1995. Through Janjalani, Yousef was able to establish an al-Qa'ida terrorist cell in the Philippines.[29]

Janjalani, however, was no mere Muslim fighter or mujahideen; he was a charismatic and a serious Muslim scholar. Born on the Philippine island of Basilan (see map), today an ASG stronghold, Janjalani (ironically) attended high school in the Catholic-run Claret College in the Basilan capital, Isabela. Though he did not finish high school, he obtained a scholarship from the government of Saudi Arabia to the Ummu I-Qura in Mecca, where he studied Islamic jurisprudence for three years.[30] Later he studied Islamic revolution in Pakistan, becoming attracted to the concept of *jihad*.

In 1984, Janjalani went back to Basilan and became an avid preacher, if to limited audiences, in the Santa Barbara madrassa in Zamboanga City. His various theological statements and public proclamations revealed a deep grasp of Islam, particularly Wahhabi theology, which considers other Muslim communities heretical. Janjalani delivered at least eight discourses, or *khutbah*, within a radical framework based on the Quranic concept of *jihad fi-sabil-lillah* (fighting and dying for the cause of Islam).[31] His discourses indicted both Muslims, even mullahs, and non-Muslims for superficial knowledge of the Quran and the Hadith (the collected tradition of Muhammad and his sayings). One of his discourses vehemently condemned the Philippine constitution as a guide for Philippine society and asserted the Quran "as the only worthy guide for human life since it is perfect creation of Allah who cannot err and who knows everything."[32] He lamented the sufferings of Muslim Filipinos as victims of oppression, injustice, and lack of development, urging them to fight and die for Islam, thus to deserve "paradise as martyrs."[33]

After his brief preaching stint in Zamboanga City, Janjalani organized a movement he called the Juma'a Abu Sayyaf, rendered in English as the Abu Sayyaf Group. The name has been mistranslated as "bearer of the sword"; it actually means "Father of the Swordsman," in reference to, and in honor of, the Afghan resistance leader Abdul Rasul Sayyaf.[34] The main objective of the ASG

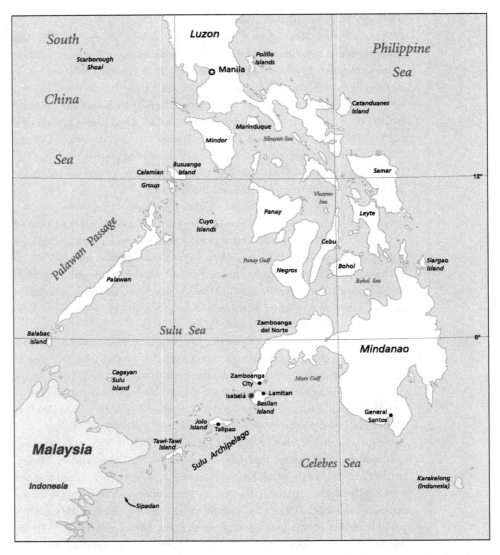

was to establish an independent theocratic Islamic state in the southern Philippines.

The struggle of ASG, like those of other Muslim radical groups in the Philippines, is deeply rooted in indigenous sociocultural, political, economic, and historical factors that can be traced to the fourteenth century.[35] In that century, seafaring Muslim traders and teachers from Indonesia and other neighboring nations reached the largely pagan Philippine Islands, spreading Islam on Mindanao and Luzon. In 1521, however, the islands were colonized for Spain by

Magellan, and the new occupiers prevented the further spread of Islam. Muslim leaders resisted the Spanish from the beginning; Filipino Muslims fought Spanish, American, and Japanese colonialism for almost four hundred years, and when the Philippines gained its independence in 1946, they continued their struggle against what they call "Imperial Manila."[36] Filipino Muslims, then, have nurtured a sense of separatism for nearly as long as Islam has existed in the Philippines.[37]

Janjalani recruited to his new movement followers from Basilan, Sulu, Tawi-Tawi, Zamboanga City, and General Santos City. Most were disgruntled former members of the Moro National Liberation Front (MNLF) or the Moro Islamic Liberation Front (MILF).

During its formative period, the ASG lacked adequate funds to advance its program. Abu Sayyaf solicited foreign funding, using the name Al Haratatul-al-Islamiya, ("Islamic movement").[38] Abu Sayyaf also engaged in kidnapping for ransom to raise funds. One of its prominent victims was Ricardo Tong, a shipyard owner, who was released on 17 January 1994 after paying a five-million-peso ransom. The ASG also conducted various extortion activities to generate funding.[39]

Structure and Membership

Janjalani envisioned a highly organized, systematic, and disciplined organization of fanatical secessionist Islamic fighters.[40] Toward this end he formed and chaired the Islamic Executive Council (IEC), composed of fifteen "amirs," heads of armed groups, as the main planning and execution body. Under the IEC were two special committees. The first committee was the Jamiatul Al-Islamia Revolutionary Tabligh Group, in charge of fund-raising and Islamic education; the second was the Al-Misuaratt Khutbah Committee, in charge of agitation and propaganda.

The ASG also formed a military arm, the Mujahidden Al-Sharifullah, composed predominantly of former members of the Moro National and Moro Islamic liberation fronts. This military arm had three main units: the Demolition Team, the Mobile Force Team, and the Campaign Propaganda Team. The Demolition Team, composed mostly of trained fighters, could manufacture its own mines and explosives. The Mobile Force Team—its members mostly affiliates of radio clubs, traders, businessmen, shippers, and professionals—was in charge of collaboration and coordination. The Campaign Propaganda Team—professionals, students, and businessmen—gathered information necessary to the mission of the Mujahidden Al-Sharifullah.

Though the fact is not widely known, the first mission of the group was a maritime operation, the bombing of a foreign missionary ship, the motor vessel

Doulous, on 10 August 1991 in Zamboanga City. The attack killed two Christian missionaries. The M/V *Doulous* bombing was a watershed event demonstrating the maritime terrorist capability of the Abu Sayyaf.

But its original organizational setup was short-lived. When the Philippine National Police and armed forces killed Janjalani in a bloody encounter in December 1998 in Lamitan, Basilan, Abu Sayyaf suffered a severe leadership vacuum, leading to the disaffection of some of its members. The organization set up by Janjalani crumbled rapidly; in particular, the IEC, once headed by Janjalani, died with him. The remaining leaders appointed Janjalani's younger brother, Khadaffi Janjalani, as his successor, but Abu Sayyaf had lost its organizational and theological cohesiveness. Most of its members resorted to banditry, piracy, and kidnapping for ransom.

The group became, and has remained, factionalized. At present, there are two major factions of the ASG operating independently in two major areas in the southern Philippines, the islands of Basilan and Sulu. Khadaffi Janjalani heads the Basilan-based faction, while Galib Andang, otherwise known as "Commander Robot," led the group on Sulu. Philippine law enforcement authorities captured Commander Robot in December 2003. He was killed in a bloody jailbreak attempt in March 2005. Other intelligence reports mention another faction operating in Zamboanga City, with Hadji Razpal as the head. But Radzpal has been identified by some intelligence sources as one of the leaders of the Sulu-based faction.

The Basilan ASG had seventy-three members as of 2002, with ten different leaders heading their own independent groups.[41] Its hard-liners comprised thirty personal followers of Khadaffi Janjalani, thirty followers of Isnillon Hapilon, and thirteen of Abu Sabaya. The group led by Hapilon was the main security arm of the Basilan ASG. Abu Sabaya's men joined the group of Khadaffi Janjalani in the daily planning and administrative affairs of the group. The Philippine military claims to have killed Sabaya and two others in June 2002. Sabaya's body was never found, however, and speculation has arisen that he may still be alive despite repeated pronouncements that Sabaya was among those who drowned in Sibuco Bay in Zamboanga del Norte.[42]

The Sulu ASG is a loose assemblage of Muslim secessionist fighters loyal to Commander Robot. As of 2002, the Sulu ASG was composed of sixteen armed groups operating independently in different areas of Sulu. This faction was responsible for the kidnapping of twenty-one tourists at a resort on Sipadan Island in Malaysia on 23 April 2000. But as stated earlier, this group lost its leader with the capture and subsequent death of Commander Robot. His capture yielded further information on the links between Abu Sayyaf and the al-Qa'ida-linked regional Islamic militant group Jemaah Islamiyah.[43]

Though ASG's main area of operation is in Mindanao, it also has attracted secret followers on Luzon, in Manila, the Philippine capital. The Rajah Solaiman Movement (RSM) is the most significant Muslim organization in Manila known to have established links with ASG. Hilarion del Rosario, Jr. (also known as Ahmed Santos) is known to have been the founder of the RSM. The group, formed in 2002, is named after the last king of Manila before the Spanish conquest in the 1500s. Most of its members are Muslim converts. Like the ASG, the converts want to remake the country as an Islamic state.[44] Reportedly, the Rajah Solaiman Movement has a special operations group and a special action force and is financed by Saudi Arabian money channeled through various charities in the Philippines. Khadaffi Janjalani allegedly gave the Rajah Solaiman Movement the equivalent of about two hundred thousand dollars for operations in Manila, which include converting Christians to Islam, then recruiting and sending them for terrorist training.[45]

ASG Strategy and Tactics

A research project of the Philippine Marine Corps asserts that Abu Sayyaf is "not basically a conventional or semi-conventional offensive unit in the strictest sense of the word."[46] Originally, Abu Sayyaf aimed to form an Islamic state, on the Taliban Afghan model, through covert guerrilla action. Today it is an organization of Muslim bandits and pirates "seeking government and international attention to claim influence and power."[47] However, its doctrine is much the same in important respects:

- Well planned operations, with high probability of success.

- High mobility and adeptness in guerrilla tactics.

- Rapport with and support from local MNLF and MILF fighters. (For major armed actions ASG seeks augmentation by active or former members of these groups, particularly those who are relatives of ASG members.)

- Dispersal, when pursued, into small groups to blend with sympathetic local civilians (often in MNLF/MILF strongholds where troops can be confused, delayed, and contained).

- Separate negotiating team in kidnaps for ransom. (The negotiation cell establishes and maintains contact with the victims' relatives; payments are either personally handed over or laundered through banks. If an entire family is held hostage—such as the Dos Palmas kidnapping—the group releases a family member to arrange ransom for the remaining members.)

- Displays of sympathy to known international terrorist organizations. Willingness to kill or injure Muslims in operations (contending that all Muslims must be willing to shed blood for the glory of Allah).

- Urban terror to divert government attention to mountain hideouts.

- Deliberate dissemination, to evade troops, of false information through commercial VHF radio and unsuspecting members of the populace.

- Kidnapping religious personalities (like Father Cirilo Nacorda, Charles Walton, and two Spanish nuns) for later release—with wide media coverage.[48]

The Basilan and Sulu groups use similar if not identical tactics.[49] Both factions employ a "water lily" strategy, a concept that aims to avoid military contact by simply sidestepping when military presence is detected and going back when troops are no longer in the area.[50]

The Threat to Maritime Security

Most ASG members and followers (regardless of faction) belong to Muslim families with strong, centuries-old seafaring traditions. Their deep knowledge of the maritime domain gives them ample capability to conduct maritime terrorism. In addition, Abu Sayyaf also possesses equipment that can be used for maritime operations. The Office of the Deputy Chief of Staff for Operations (DCSO-J3) of the Armed Forces of the Philippines (AFP) reports that it has used night-vision devices, thermal imagers, sniper scopes, various types of commercial radio, satellites, cellular phones, and high-speed water craft.[51] Further, ASG has a proven ability to establish linkages with like-minded terrorist groups in Southeast Asia. One of them in particular, the Moro Islamic Liberation Front, has seaborne resources that can be harnessed for maritime terrorism. MILF demonstrated its maritime terrorist capability in February 2000, when it attacked the vessel *Our Lady Mediatrix,* killing forty persons and wounding fifty.[52]

The explosion of *Superferry 14,* carrying 899 passengers, on 27 February 2004 put the ASG in the spotlight. The tragedy claimed nearly a hundred lives. The Philippine government officially denied that Abu Sayyaf had been involved; President Gloria Macapagal Arroyo issued a statement dismissing speculation that ASG had masterminded the incident. But an ASG spokesperson, Abu Soliman, insisted that Abu Sayyaf was indeed responsible, claiming that the attack was revenge for violence in Mindanao.[53] Soliman identified "passenger 51," Arnulfo Alvarado (a pseudonym of Redento Cain Dellosa), as the bomber. Khadaffi Janjalani confirmed Soliman's claim and warned the Philippine government that Abu Sayyaf's "best action" was yet to come.[54]

A Marine Board of Inquiry that investigated the incident ultimately confirmed that Abu Sayyaf attacked *Superferry 14.*[55] Former Philippine national security adviser Norberto Gonzales has stated in an interview that "because of the nature of the wreck, half-submerged in the bay, it will be difficult for investigators to prove 100% that it was Abu Sayyaf. But the overwhelming evidence points that way, and I'm certain they were the ones behind the attack."[56] On 10 October 2004, the Philippine government finally concurred that the ASG had planted the bomb that sank *Superferry 14*.[57] Presumably it was the work of the Basilan faction with the assistance of the RSM. Redento Cain Dellosa, an RSM member, confessed during police interrogation that he had planted a bomb on the ferry.

Plainly, Abu Sayyaf, once a predominantly land-based terrorist organization, is becoming more and more maritime in its operations, to escape the predominantly land-based Philippine military responses to internal security threats.[58]

The Philippine government in 2002 described Abu Sayyaf as a "spent force." Nonetheless, the ASG has apparently become more innovative in its terrorist tactics not only in the Philippines but in neighboring countries of Southeast Asia, particularly in Malaysia and Indonesia. In a telephone interview about the *Superferry 14* incident, Soliman taunted the Philippine government: "Still doubtful about our capabilities? Good. Just wait and see. We will bring the war that you impose on us to your lands and seas, homes, and streets. We will multiply the pain and suffering that you have inflicted on our people."[59] Indeed, the capability of ASG to wage maritime terrorism should not be underestimated. Intelligence reports indicate that it can still exploit Islam to recruit members and solicit support. Its cellular structure makes detection difficult; thus, it can still launch terrorist acts far from its traditional areas of operation. The ASG is also highly elusive, due to its maritime capability and experience.

Abu Sayyaf has an extensive history of maritime terrorist attacks. Two have already been mentioned: the 1991 bombing of the M/V *Doulous* and the 2000 kidnapping of tourists on Sipadan.[60] A few months later, on 30 September 2000, ASG kidnapped three Malaysians in Pasir Beach Resort in Sabah using a speedboat. The April 2000 kidnapping ended only in 2001, when the ASG reportedly received a fifteen-million-dollar ransom from the Philippine government.[61] The September 2000 kidnapping was resolved more quickly; Philippine troops rescued the three Malaysians in Talipao, Sulu.

On 27 May 2001, the ASG waged another act of maritime terror when it abducted three American citizens and seventeen Filipinos at the Dos Palmas resort on Palawan. This act can be considered a maritime attack, because the target was a maritime area—a beach resort. Some ASG members involved in the incident were disguised as diving instructors. The incident received international coverage, because several of the victims, including an American citizen, were murdered and beheaded. During a rescue operation mounted by the Filipino government in 2002, two victims, one of them a U.S. citizen, were killed.[62] The Dos Palmas incident was a wake-up call for the United States.[63] The result was a controversial joint operation in 2002, BALIKATAN 02-1, aimed at destroying Abu Sayyaf.[64] BALIKATAN 02-1 resulted in the neutralization of many ASG members, including, as noted, the reported death of Abu Sabaya and the eventual capture and death of the Sulu faction leader, Commander Robot.

Nonetheless, to generate funds in an attempt to recover from the impact of BALIKATAN 02-1, in September 2003 Abu Sayyaf threatened to hijack vessels of the Sulpicio and WG&A lines. In April 2004, just two months after the *Superferry 14* incident, the ASG kidnapped two Malaysians and an Indonesian in a sailing craft. By this time the Philippine Coast Guard was considering the Philippines increasingly under threat of maritime terrorism.[65] Manila has identified twenty-six ports and anchorages vulnerable to such maritime terrorist attacks.[66]

THE PHILIPPINE RESPONSE TO MARITIME TERRORISM

In its 2003 annual report of accomplishments, the Philippine Department of National Defense (DND) reported 117 armed engagements with Abu Sayyaf. Of them, eighty had been initiated by the Philippine forces, the rest by the ASG—twenty in ASG guerrilla operations, seventeen in terrorist activities. The DND reported the neutralization of 174 ASG members—eighty killed (including Father Roman Al-Ghozi, an international terrorist linked to the group), seventeen captured, three surrendered, and seventy-four apprehended. In that year Philippine forces also arrested Commander Robot and rescued all kidnapped victims in 2003, including four Indonesian hostages. The Philippine armed forces aimed to reduce Abu Sayyaf strength to less than one hundred, from 461, by the end of 2004.[67] But Abu Sayyaf's strength has only been cut to 380, as of the second quarter of 2005. Nonetheless, the Department of National Defense reports that "the ASG is presently factionalized and its remnants have splintered and are constantly on the move due to continued military pressures."[68]

Notwithstanding this drastic reduction in numerical strength, Abu Sayyaf continues to be a maritime threat, "a group we must monitor closely, not only because it might desire to strike the broader maritime sector, but because its membership includes well equipped, highly trained fighters with significant experience in both day and night maritime combat operations."[69] Addressing this threat will require a strengthening of the intelligence capability of law enforcement agencies in the Philippines. A sound intelligence system is a vital component of any counterterrorism strategy, whether land-based or maritime, as a source of information on the nature of terrorist groups, the threat they represent, and their intentions, capabilities, and opportunities.[70] Accurate and reliable intelligence may in fact be the most effective weapon against terrorism, enabling "operational agencies and law enforcement authorities to develop measures to detect a terrorist threat at the planning and preparation phases."[71]

Philippine military officials, however, admit that the nation has a very weak intelligence network. Despite Administrative Order 68, issued by the government on 8 April 2003 to strengthen the National Intelligence Coordinating Agency (NICA), state intelligence capability remains weak. A former armed forces chief of staff, General Narciso Abaya, has candidly acknowledged that the nonsharing of intelligence information is hampering the government's antiterrorism campaign.[72] Abaya believes that a culture exists among intelligence units in the Philippines to withhold vital intelligence information: "I think we have to improve on our intelligence. The trend now is not the need to know but the need to share. That is the emerging trend among intelligence units all over the world."[73] In fact, he lamented, "sometimes, our intelligence units zealously keep to themselves intelligence information that, if fused with the information of other intelligence units, would give a more comprehensive picture of the enemy."[74]

There have also been serious allegations that the military and provincial governments are coddling Abu Sayyaf. The International Peace Mission that went to Basilan on 23–27 March 2002 reported that "there are consistent credible reports that the military and the provincial government are coddling the Abu Sayyaf."[75] In such circumstances a military approach "will not work to solve the problem."[76] As early as 1994, in fact, there were charges that police and fake police officers were involved in an ASG attempt to smuggle firearms into Zamboanga City from Manila and Iloilo on board the motor vessel *Princess of the Pacific*. The police and the military authorities insist that connivance with ASG is not being tolerated and that those found guilty of it will be punished.

Nonetheless, the Philippine military recognizes that a military solution alone cannot defeat Abu Sayyaf. An after-action report of the ASG Combat Research and Study Group of the Training and Doctrine Command of the Philippine Army submitted on 19 September 2001 to the commanding general of the Army states:

> The ASG problem cannot be solved through military solution alone. It should be approached by complementary and mutually reinforcing efforts by the civil agencies and the military. The government must concretely pursue social, economic and political reforms aimed at addressing the root causes of the problem. Effective measures must also be undertaken to ensure the welfare and protection of civilians and reduce the impact of the armed conflict on them. These should necessarily include intensified delivery of basic services to conflict areas.[77]

In other words, the Abu Sayyaf threat needs a comprehensive and holistic approach. To that end the Philippine government established the Cabinet Oversight Committee on International Security (COCIS). COCIS uses what is known as the "strategy of holistic approach" (SHA) to overcome insurgency problems in the Philippines generally. The SHA has four major components: political, legal, and diplomatic; socioeconomic and psychosocial; peace, order, and security; and information.

The political/legal/diplomatic component of the SHA envisions political reforms and institutional development to strengthen democratic institutions and empower the citizenry to pursue personal and community growth. This component aims to develop and propagate Philippine democracy to confront the communist and Islamic fundamentalist ideology. Its cornerstone is a process based on "Six Paths to Peace":

- Pursuit of social, economic, and political reforms

- Consensus building and empowerment for peace

- Peaceful, negotiated settlement with rebel groups

- Programs for reconciliation, reintegration, and rehabilitation

- Conflict management and protection of civilians caught in armed conflict

- Construction and nurturing of a climate conducive to peace.

The socioeconomic/psychosocial component of the holistic approach, for its part, aims to alleviate poverty in the country through the acceleration of development programs of the Philippine government. It also set out to develop and strengthen a spirit of nationhood among the people, by developing national character/identity without loss of cultural integrity. The peace and order/security component is designed to protect the people from the insurgents and provide a secure environment for national development. More importantly, this component has the specific goal of denying the insurgents "access to their most important resource—popular support." Finally, the information component integrates the SHA. It "refers to the overall effort to advocate peace, promote public confidence in government and support government efforts to overcome insurgency through tri-media and interpersonal approaches."

The operational aspect of the holistic approach is of a dual nature. President Arroyo explains, "How do we address this problem [of] insurgency? Through the right-hand and left-hand approach. [The] right hand is the full force of the law and the left hand is the hand of reconciliation and the hand of giving support to our poorest brothers so that they won't be encouraged to join the rebels."[78]

While the SHA is meant to primarily combat communist insurgency, it is also being applied to terrorist threats.[79] The Philippine government disestablished COCIS in October 2004 and transferred its related responsibilities to the Anti-Terrorism Task Force (ATTF), which had been formed on 24 March 2004.

The ATTF is presently the central government body responsible for strategies, policies, plans, and measures to prevent and suppress terrorism in the Philippines, particularly by Abu Sayyaf.

The ATTF's main operations, however, are predominantly land based rather than maritime, and in general it is too early to assess the effectiveness of SHA in countering Abu Sayyaf. According to its own reports, however, from March to June 2004 the ATTF killed fourteen ASG members, captured fourteen, and arrested twenty-nine others.[80] Through the ATTF, the Philippine government in October 2004 charged six suspected ASG members with responsibility for the *Superferry 14* attack. Two, believed to have planted the bomb, are in police custody; four others, including Khadaffi Janjalani and Abu Soliman, remain at large.[81]

To deal with the maritime terrorist threat posed by Abu Sayyaf, it is imperative that the Philippine government strengthen its intelligence capacity. Still, intelligence is a short-term remedy; a long-term solution requires addressing root causes. The root causes of Abu Sayyaf's struggle are comprehensive and multidimensional—if most of its original members have resorted to banditry and piracy, there are others who adhere to its original religious aim—and therefore so must be the state response.

The "strategy of holistic approach" is an attempt to operationalize that necessity. However, the operations it has generated are predominantly on land. Moreover, its success will depend on the extent to which the Philippine government can win the hearts and minds of the people, particularly those in areas vulnerable to terrorist agitation and propaganda.

The Philippine government cannot address this growing threat alone. It needs the cooperation of other sectors from the civil society and nongovernmental organizations. It also needs the cooperation of like-minded regional states. Only sustained interagency, intersociety, and interstate cooperation can effectively address the maritime terrorist threat posed by Abu Sayyaf.

NOTES

1. Steven Rogers, "Manila Must Counter the Return of the Abu Sayyaf," *International Herald Tribune*, 20 May 2004.

2. This section draws upon the author's "Maritime Security Outlook for Southeast Asia" (paper presented at the Maritime Security Conference organized by the Institute of Defence and Strategic Studies, Singapore, 20–21 May 2004). It appears in Joshua Ho and Catherine Zara Raymond, eds., *The Best of Times, the Worst of Times: Maritime Security in the Asia Pacific* (Singapore: World Scientific, 2005).

3. International Chambers of Commerce, "Annual Death Toll from Piracy Rises," 7 February

2005, available at www.iccwbo.org/home/news_archives/2005/2004_piracy.asp.

4. Tamara Renee Shie, "Ports in a Storm? The Nexus between Counterterrorism, Counter-proliferation, and Maritime Security in Southeast Asia," *Issues and Insights* 4, no. 4 (July 2004), p. 13.

5. Patrick Goodenough, "Maritime Security Takes Center Stage in SE Asia," CNSNews.com, 29 June 2004, www.cnsnews.com/. Also see Rubert Herbert-Burns and Lauren Zucker, "Malevolent Tide: Fusion and Overlaps in Piracy and Maritime Terrorism" (Washington, D.C.: Maritime Intelligence Group, 30 July 2004), p. 1.

6. Richard Halloran, "Link between Terrorists, Pirates in SE Asia a Growing Concern," HonoluluAdvertiser.com, 7 March 2004, the.honoluluadvertiser.com/article/2004/Mar/07.

7. Tanner Campbell and Rohan Gunaratna, "Maritime Terrorism, Piracy and Crime," in *Terrorism in the Asia Pacific: Threat and Response,* ed. Rohan Gunaratna (Singapore: Eastern Univ. Press, 2003), p. 72.

8. Office of Naval Intelligence, *Threats and Challenges to Maritime Security 2020* (Washington, D.C.: U.S. Coast Guard Intelligence Coordination Center, 1 March 1999), chap. 3, available at www.fas.org/irp/threat/maritime2020/CHAPTER3.htm.

9. Ibid.

10. H. R. Vitasa and Nararya Soeprapto, "Maritime Sector Developments in ASEAN" (paper presented in the Maritime Policy Seminar organized by the United Nations Conference on Trade and Development and the Ministry of Communications of Indonesia, Jakarta, 11–13 October 1999).

11. For a good reference see John Noer and David Gregory, *Chokepoints: Maritime Economic Concerns in Southeast Asia* (Washington, D.C.: National Defense Univ., 1996).

12. U.S. Pacific Command, "Shipping and Commerce," www.pacom.mil/publications/apeu02/s04ship7.pdf.

13. Zachary Abuza, "Terrorism in Southeast Asia: Keeping al-Qaeda at Bay," *Terrorism Monitor* 2, no. 9 (6 May 2004), p. 5.

14. Joshua Ho, of the Singapore-based Institute of Defence and Strategic Studies, gave this analysis in an interview with the *Economist:* "Shipping in Southeast: Going for the Jugular," *Economist,* 10 June 2004, available at www.economist.com/World/asia/displayStory.cfm?story_id=2752802.

15. Michael Richardson, *A Time Bomb for Global Trade: Maritime-Related Terrorism in the Age of Weapons of Mass Destruction* (Singapore: Institute of Southeast Asian Studies, 2004).

16. This is the main theme of the session "The Terrorist Threat to the Maritime Sector in Southeast Asia and the Straits of Malacca" at the International Maritime and Port Security Conference held in Singapore on 4–5 August 2004 [hereafter International Conference].

17. John F. Bradford, "Maritime Terror in Southeast Asia: Will the Fire Spread in a Region Already Ablaze?" (paper presented at the International Conference).

18. "First Sea Lord Warns of Al-Qaeda Plot to Target Merchant Ships," *FREE Lloyd's List Daily News Bulletin,* 5 August 2004, www.lloydslist.com/bulletin.

19. Associated Press, "Expert: Al-Qa'ida Planning Seaborne Attack," Fox News Channel, 17 March 2004. Also see "Al-Qa'ida Planning Seaborne Attack," Fox News Channel, 17 March 2004, www.foxnews.com.

20. Abuza, "Terrorism in Southeast Asia," p. 5.

21. See "Al-Qaida Plans High-Sea Terror," WorldNetDaily, 13 October 2003, www.worldnetdaily.com/news/printer-friendly.asp?ARTICLE_ID=35047.

22. Goodenough, "Maritime Security Takes Center Stage in SE Asia," p. 2.

23. Halloran, "Link between Terrorists, Pirates in SE Asia a Growing Concern," p. 1.

24. Agence France Presse, "Piracy Equals Terrorism on Troubled Waters: Minister," 21 Singapore 2003.

25. Ibid.

26. See, for example, Rommel C. Banlaoi, *War on Terrorism in Southeast Asia* (Quezon City, R.P.: Rex Book Store International, 2004); Maria Ressa, *Seeds of Terror: An Eyewitness Account of Al-Qaeda's Newest Center of Operations in Southeast Asia* (New York: Free Press, 2003); Djanicelle J. Berreveld, *Terrorism in*

the Philippines: The Bloody Trail of Abu Sayyaf, Bin Laden's East Asian Connection (San Jose, Calif.: Writers Club, 2001); and Zachary Abuza, "Tentacles of Terror: Al-Qaeda's Southeast Asian Network," Contemporary Southeast Asia 24, no. 3 (December 2002), pp. 427–65.

27. For an insightful analysis on the evolution of ASG, see Rohan Gunaratna, "The Evolution and Tactics of the Abu Sayyaf Group," Jane's Intelligence Review (July 2001). For an excellent historical analysis, see Graham H. Turbiville, Jr., "Bearer of the Sword," Military Review (March/April 2002), pp. 38–47.

28. For discussion see Mehol K. Sadain, Global and Regional Trends in Islamic Resurgence: Their Implications on the Southern Philippines (Pasay City, R.P.: Foreign Service Institute, 1994).

29. For a detailed account, see Rohan Gunaratna, Inside Al-Qaeda: Global Network of Terror (New York: Columbia Univ. Press, 2002).

30. Glenda Gloria, "Bearer of the Sword: The Abu Sayyaf Has Nebulous Beginnings and Incoherent Aims," Mindanao Updates, 6 June 2000, www.pcij.org/mindanao/abusayyaf.html.

31. Samuel K. Tan, "The Juma'a Abu Sayyaf: A Brief Assessment of Its Origin, Objectives, Ideology and Method of Struggle" (draft, unpublished manuscript, 24 April 2000), p. 3.

32. Ibid.

33. Ibid.

34. Jose Torres, Jr., Into the Mountain: Hostages by the Abu Sayyaf (Quezon City, R.P.: Claretian, 2001), p. 35.

35. See Andrew Tan, "The Indigenous Roots of Conflict in Southeast Asia: The Case of Mindanao," in After Bali: The Threat of Terrorism in Southeast Asia, ed. Kumar Ramakrishna and See Seng Tan (Singapore: Institute of Defence and Strategic Studies, 2003), pp. 97–116.

36. For excellent studies on the Muslim problem, see T. J. S. George, Revolt in Mindanao: The Rise of Islam in Philippine Politics (New York: Oxford Univ. Press, 1980); Cesar A. Majul, The Contemporary Muslim Movement in the Philippines (Berkeley, Calif.: Mizan, 1985); Peter Gowing, Mosque and Moro: A Study of

Muslims in the Philippines (Manila: Federation of Christian Churches, 1964); and Cesar Majul, Muslim in the Philippines (Quezon City: Univ. of the Philippines Press, 1973).

37. Catharin E. Dalpino, "Separatism and Terrorism in the Philippines: Distinctions and Options for U.S. Policy," testimony before the Subcommittee on East Asia and the Pacific, House International Relations Committee of the U.S. Congress, 10 June 2003, p. 2.

38. Janjalani got this name from Al-Haraka, an international organization of Muslim fundamentalists, mostly radicals and amirs like Janjalani, based in Pakistan and headed by Sibani Juruz Talib. Al-Haraka envisions the reshaping of the Islamic world through global jihad. Philippine Department of National Defense, Info Kit on the Abu Sayyaf Group (August 2001).

39. Philippine Department of National Defense, Abu Sayyaf Group Reference Folder (17 November 2003).

40. This section is based largely on the following sources: Office of the Deputy Chief of Staff for Operations, J3, Knowing the Terrorists: The Abu Sayyaf Study (Quezon City: Headquarters of the Armed Forces of the Philippines, n.d.); and Office of the Assistant to the Chief of Staff for Intelligence, Field Handout: Doctrinal Extract for the Abu Sayyaf Group (Headquarters of the Philippine Marine Corps, 21 January 2002).

41. For further discussion, see the author's "Leadership Dynamics in Terrorist Organizations in Southeast Asia: The Abu Sayyaf Case" (paper presented at the international symposium "The Dynamics and Structures of Terrorist Threats in Southeast Asia," organized by the Institute of Defense Analyses in cooperation with the Southeast Asia Regional Center for Counter-Terrorism and U.S. Pacific Command, Kuala Lumpur, Malaysia, 18–20 April 2005).

42. "Sabaya's Death Not the End of Abu Sayyaf, says Basilan Bishop," MindaNews, 29 June 2002, www.mindanews.com/2002/07/1st/nws29abu.html. According to a friend of the author, a member of the Special Warfare Group, which carried out the operation, Sabaya was indeed killed in the battle.

43. "Commander Robot's Capture Big Blow to Abu Sayyaf," *Sun Star*, 8 December 2003, at www.sunstar.com.ph/static/net/2003/12/08/commander.robot.s.capture.big.blow.to.abu.sayyaf.(12.31.p.m.).html.

44. Joe Cochrane, "Filipino Authorities Say the Newest Threat to the Country Is a Shadowy Terror Group Made Up of Radical Muslim Converts," *Newsweek International Edition*, 17 May 2004, msnbc.msn.com/id/4933472/; *Summary of Report on Rajah Solaiman Movement*, 12 April 2004, www.westerndefense.org/articles/PhilippineRepublic/may04.htm.

45. *Summary of Report on Rajah Solaiman Movement*.

46. Office of the Assistant to the Chief of Staff for Intelligence, *Field Handout*, p. 17.

47. Ibid.

48. *Info Kit on the Abu Sayyaf Group*, pp. 5–6.

49. Office of the Deputy Chief of Staff for Operations, J3, *Knowing the Terrorists*, p. 27.

50. Ibid.

51. Ibid., p. 12.

52. Campbell and Gunaratna, "Maritime Terrorism, Piracy and Crime," p. 77.

53. Teresa Cerojano, "Said Bomber aboard Philippines Ferry," Associated Press, 2 March 2004, www.boston.com/news/world/asia/articles/2004/03/02/said_bomber_aboard_philippines_ferry/.

54. "Philippines Ferry Explosion: Terror or Accident," editorial, *Philippine Daily Inquirer*, 2 March 2004.

55. Author interview, August 2004.

56. Simon Elegant, "The Return of the Abu Sayyaf," *Time Asia*, 30 August 2004, www.time.com/time/asia/magazine/article/0,13673,501040830-686107,00.html.

57. "Abu Sayyaf Planted bomb in 'Superferry,' Says GMA," *Manila Times*, 12 October 2004, www.manilatimes.net/national/2004/oct/12/yehey/top_stories/20041012to.

58. Land-based terrorist attacks of ASG have been documented by Mark Turner, "Terrorism and Secession in the Southern Philippines: The Rise of the Abu Sayyaf," *Contemporary Southeast Asia* 17, no. 1 (June 1995), pp. 1–19.

59. Marco Garrido, "After Madrid, Manila?" *Asia Times*, 24 April 2004, www.atimes.com/atimes/Southeast_Asia/FD24Ae01.html; Manny Mogato, "The Abu Sayyaf Group: No Religious Revolutionaries, Just Bandits Pure and Simple," Cyberdyaryo.com, www.cyberdyaryo.com/features/f2001_0615_01.htm.

60. Peter Chalk, "Separatism and Southeast Asia: The Islamic Factor in Southern Thailand, Mindanao, and Aceh," *Studies in Conflict and Terrorism* 24, no. 4 (1 July 2001).

61. For an eyewitness account of the issue including the controversial payment of ransom, see Roberto N. Aventajado, *140 Days of Terror: In the Clutches of the Abu Sayyaf* (Pasig City, R.P.: Anvil, 2004).

62. Gracia Burnham and Dean Merrill, *In the Presence of My Enemies* (Wheaton, Ill.: Tyndale House, 2003).

63. Larry Niksch, *Abu Sayyaf: Target of Philippine-U.S. Anti-Terrorism Cooperation*, CRS Report for Congress (Washington, D.C.: Congressional Research Service, 25 January 2002).

64. See Rommel C. Banlaoi, "The Role of Philippine-American Relations in the Global Campaign against Terrorism: Implications for Regional Security," *Contemporary Southeast Asia* 24, no. 2 (August 2002), pp. 294–312, and "Philippine-American Security Relations and the War on Terrorism in Southeast Asia," in *International Relations of the Asia Pacific after 9/11 and China's Accession to WTO*, ed. Wang Xingsheng (Guangzhou, PRC: Zhongshan Univ. Institute of Southeast Asian Studies, 2003), pp. 80–95.

65. Agence France-Presse, "Philippines Seen Increasingly under Threat from Maritime Terrorism," 8 September 2003, quickstart.clari.net/qs_se/webnews/wed/ao/Qphilippines-apec-attacks.RBWM_DS8.html.

66. Ibid.

67. Office of the Assistant Secretary for Plans and Programs, *Annual Accomplishment Report of the Department of National Defense for 2003* (Quezon City, R.P.: Department of National Defense, 2004).

68. Department of National Defense, *Defense Planning Guide, 2006-2011* (Quezon City: Department of National Defense Office of the

Undersecretary for Policy, Plans and Special Concerns, December 2004).

69. Bradford, "Maritime Terror in Southeast Asia," p. 8. Also see "Expert: Dire Warning on Threat of Maritime Terrorism," *Star Online,* 16 August 2004, 202.186.86.35/maritime/story.asp?file=/2004/8/16/maritime/8656995&sec=maritime.

70. Campbell and Gunaratna, "Maritime Terrorism, Piracy and Crime," p. 86.

71. Rohan Gunaratna, "Terrorism and Small Arms and Light Weapons," in *Terrorism and Disarmament,* Occasional Paper 5 (n.p.: Department of Disarmament Affairs, October 2001), p. 54.

72. Karl B. Kaufman, "'Weak' Intel Blamed on Overzealous Spy Units," *Manila Times,* 26 March 2004, www.manilatimes.net/national/2004/mar/26/yehey/top_stories/20040326top6.html.

73. Ibid.

74. Ibid.

75. For a complete copy of the report, see *Basilan: The Next Afghanistan?* Report of the International Peace Mission to Basilan, Philippines, 23–27 March 2002, available at www.bwf.org/pamayanan/peacemission.html.

76. Ibid.

77. ASG Combat Research and Study Group, "After Action Report" (submitted to the commanding general of the Philippine Army on 19 September 2001 by the Training and Doctrine Command).

78. Marichu Villanueva, "Palace Announces RP-CPP Peace Talks Resume in Oslo February 10–13," *The Philippine Star* (6 February 2004), www.newsflash.org/2003/05/hl/hl019815.htm.

79. Department of National Defense, *Talking Points on Abu Sayyaf Group* (Quezon City, R.P.: Office of the Assistant Secretary for Plans and Programs, 17 November 2003). This document explains the use of SHA in countering the ASG.

80. Inter-Agency Anti-Terrorism Task Force, Accomplishment Report (Manila: March–June 2004).

81. Lira Dalangin-Fernandez, "6 Abu Sayyaf Militants Charged for Ferry Bombing," *Philippine Daily Inquirer,* 11 October 2004, news.inq7.net/top/index.php?index=1&story_id=14549.

CPSIA information can be obtained
at www.ICGtesting.com
Printed in the USA
BVHW060928090821
613980BV00013BA/502